Dear Sue,
Hope you like
All th
Mark

Tin Cat Alley

by

Mark Murphy

SPOUT Publications
1996

Published by Spout Publications
Birstall Library
Market Street
Birstall, Batley
West Yorkshire WF17 9EN

Typeset at The Word Hoard

Printed by Peepal Tree Press, Leeds

ISBN 1 899114 16 5

Spout Publications exists to publish writers involved in writing workshops and projects run by The Word Hoard, the literature development agency based in the Borough of Kirklees, West Yorkshire.

We do not consider unsolicited manuscripts.

Spout Publications gratefully acknowledges the financial assistance of Kirklees Metropolitan Council and Yorkshire and Humberside Arts Board.

Acknowledgments are due to the following publications, in which some of these poems first appeared:
First Draft (The Albert Poets), *Spout, The Wide Skirt, Huddersfield University Unity Festival Against Discrimination Programme 1995.*

Contents

The Lead Cat

I am the quintessence of the age.
I am the lead cat.
I am not afraid to speak my mind.

Stand up, I say, stand up
for what you believe in
if you believe in anything at all.

No matter that it is no longer
fashionable to do so,
that it offends certain

sensibilities. *Ladies and gentlemen!*
Hold on to your carrots!
No matter that talk of goodies

and baddies is considered purely
subjective, or, for that matter, that what's said
is not even listened to

And no matter (especially so)
that what's said
is not considered poetry.

Fate, or rather, the iceberg, has dealt
us a cruel blow, the cruellest
blow of all. *Here's your last chance!*

No matter (even now) that what's
what isn't necessarily
what it seems.

As the ship goes down
and the final eulogies
are spoken, each must face

the inevitable
gurgling; weighing on the mind
like lead.

Din. Din. Din. Din. Din.
What a ridiculous notion,
a ship made of tin.

for Bruno S.

...So your car's kaput,
and your girlfriend has gone,
and thine house they have sold...

It is important for poets to talk about loss
            in their poetry
whether it be lost love, the loss of reason, or the loss of hair.
We might observe, then, that losing, by whatever margin,
is fundamental, not just for poets, but for all of us.
By the same token, without loss, nothing can be gained.
A penny that is never lost, can never be found.
A man who has never lost at poker, will only know
what it is like to win. In virtue of this, he has lost out
            on what it is to lose.

Alas! the balding man pipes up, anxious to be heard,
posing his question, before any eventuality of him losing
his thread: *But does all loss have equal weight?*
And we must do him the decency of addressing
his enquiry; after all, to the balding man, hair loss
might signify the loss of youth, virility, or even his position
in the world. For him, the experience of balding
might well be commensurate with our horror
at the fat woman on the cliff face (an inexperienced climber)
who, by some misfortune, has lost her footing
and now dangles by her own unfortunate shoelaces.
Even as I relate her story, the audience will voice
their dissent. *Dolt! Dullard! Dunderhead!*
Has she completely lost her marbles!

            As for the man who has never lost out
            in love,
            we might well conjecture, that he too is lost.

The Untrodden Snow

A girl in the pub thinks I'm a poet.
She asks me what I do.
I tell her I notice things,
like her mouth, its thick lips.
She says it isn't good enough
and wants to know what poets do.
She has her own ideas.

Mainly they live in lofts,
eat baked beans
straight from the tin,
drink a lot and can be seen
more often than not walking
in town parks. She says
it's all part of her job.

I was drunk, walked
home through the park,
didn't see any poets there,
didn't see anybody,
just snow drifting
this way and that, and a dog
barking up a tree.

Last night, when I got home
I fell in the snow.
It was as if I hadn't noticed
it before. Except
for one bathroom light - the outline
of a man and a woman showering
the whole street was in darkness.

The snow was all mine.
It felt good
thinking about the girl in the pub.

How pretty she was. Her big eyes.
Her mouth when she smiled.
Her laugh when she said
I think poets are supposed to write poetry.

Manageable Space

Anyone acquainted with
the ideas of Herr Freud
will be glad to learn

as I did
that we are not alone
in our anxieties;

even the good
professor suffered
bouts of agoraphobia,

which is no laughing matter
since the response
is one of terror.

Asked what it was
that caused the fear
he might've said

it was his childhood,
an early memory of steam
trains, the action

of the pistons, or
that the rattling
of the carriage mimicked

death. Imagine then,
a lake reservoir -
nothing too disturbing.

You need to get away
from the water, the expanse
is too much, too blue.

You need to get back
to the world
of enclosure, the world

of manageable space.
Now imagine Sigmund's train.
On such journeys

the reasonable world is lost
to the opening out
of an unfamiliar landscape;

where the desire to get free
is contradicted
by the desire to hide.

Mousetrap

She doesn't look very happy
standing there in the rain.

I feel uncomfortable watching
her through the blinds.

I've got things to do, besides
she doesn't need my sympathy.

Maybe I should call to her,
lend her an umbrella.

You'd think she'd have one
dressed like that in the rain.

Then again, it wouldn't do;
it would spoil the look.

I mean, who'd be interested
in a girl trying to keep dry.

Fragile Spring

The chinese flower-seller
is selling spring
in pubs and clubs
at all night parties

to couples in stifled rooms
who are eager
the boys to give
girls to receive
a bit of spring.

She tells them
words are not enough-
flowers are needed.

Yes, it's spring
she's selling
on city streets
in urban gardens,
emptied of feeling.

And the lovers who are falling
they are not alone
grasping at fragile spring...

Crocuses! Daffodils! Tulips!

Notes from Prison

for Osip Mandelstam

I read your poetry at night.
I am a big fan.
But what of the oppositionists at Vorkuta?
Who will write for us?

You are insistent;
St Petersburg is a grave for the intelligentsia.
But the whole of Russia is a grave.
What of the opposition at Vorkuta?

There're no graves to keep clean
only shots resounding in the tundra.
The sound of departing feet.
Who will sing our song?

I speak to you after years of silence;
we have gone beyond poetry.
It is useless to write it here,
the world won't accept truth, any truth.

Nothing is plain anymore;
at least, this is what we're told.
Osip Emilievich, I know your darkness
I have lived it in my own little way.

Night Bird

From this room there's no telling
what I can see, the dereliction
of mills is only part of it;
too familiar to be considered
important by passing buses or cars.
Go tell it to Oscar or Nancy
or hundreds more who inhabit the rafters
where air vents are secretive
like hooded monks mumbling prayers.

I've lived in many rooms, but none
like this, none as revealing as this;
as usual, the moon has nothing to say
but I can see the moods of light
with the eye of an artist tracing
the dark eye of the sun, spires
aspiring to the insoluble, and jets
climbing through the shepherd's warning.

Believe me, night after night
without sleep's not easy, alcohol
only leaves the brain bloated
with worry, head down facing the vomit
and self defeat, and the early
morning sky plays tricks so cruel,
they go unnoticed by the untrained eye.

Though the sky round here is polluted
with neon, I've dispensed with curtains;
they only keep in the dark.

Fly Story

The fly in the fly bottle won't play today.
Perhaps it's too hot. Everybody knows
it's not good to be cooped up in such heat.

Even the boy crawls under the iron bedstead
to where it's cool. From there he can hear
his parents shouting, but doesn't listen.

He's proud of his captive, but can't help
wishing it was a butterfly, better still
a caterpillar; if only he could catch another
to keep it company, to keep it from dying.

He hits the bottle with a rusty nail,
and bangs it against the skirtings.
It's not fair having to be in for nine.

His mother shouts for him to get to bed.
School in the morning and something about
a bloody good hiding. Like last time.

He stops. What if the bottle breaks?
The fly doesn't move. He taps the bottle
with the nail and waits. The weather's hot,
the night undisturbed. Not even a breeze.

Years later he recounts the story drunk
to the woman he's living with. She's upset
by his lateness. He crawls into bed.
She can't go on like this. He doesn't move.

Notes from the Aparatchick's Desk

The new regime has ordered the removal
of Vladimir Ilych from all public places.
He is no longer regarded as a friend;
from now on, we shall refer to him as Lenin,
less than human, a monster like Stalin.

The remaining portraits are to be taken
from all gvt premises and incinerated.
The portraits of President Yeltsin
will replace them. Statues should be
dismantled, by force if necessary.

Certain books will have to be burnt.
No point arguing. Certain books
will always have to be burnt.
It is a busy time for the new bureaucracy,
the renaming of parts is not for mugs.

A spade is no longer a spade.
It is a shovel. Gvt. directive no. 5.
Laugh at us and you will be disqualified
from entering the state lottery.
Laugh with us and fortune will surely be yours.

In our efforts to rediscover the past,
the Lenin Brain Institute
will have to close. You will remember
we do all this, not out of love,
but in the name of progress.

The new authorities have revealed
that Lenin's brain was only marginally
bigger than average. A matter of ounces.
It is hardly surprising, then, that
70 years of research have been in vain.

The Tobogganist

I'm finished

with God. I never wanted to be
favoured anyway. It's not a question
of faith, being abandoned or even fallenness
from being; *Dasein's* only another way
out, an abstract prop, improvisation
for the stage. Let me tell you

being encased in ice is not much fun,
too much time to think, obsession
with death's nothing
new, only gets you down; it's remembering
always remembering, the mountain
doesn't concern itself with the weight

of the avalanche. Don't get me wrong
I embrace the physicality of the world,
and though it's dark down here
I dream a lot; sometimes I dream
of monasteries in altitudes where the air is thin;
I have questions of uncertainty for them.

Being well versed in the doctrine
of eventualities only hampers the process.
Nevertheless, I dream of girls
and lots of them too, but the best
times come in quieter moments
when I think I can see the winter sun climbing

among peaks and glaciers.

September in Paris

September rain fingering the cobbles outside the Café Dome.
The night air suffused with the smell of tomorrow's bread.
The city full of couples being couples.

Already I'm lying, but the lie pleases, because the lie is all
that's left. I can't help myself. Call it selfishness, human failing,
my particular failing; the need to know, now given to doubt,
lies blind behind the eyes, thirsts for answers.

The nights are no longer than they ever were, just less
involved. All the same, the sky tonight is heavy with clouds.
And my reaction is agoraphobic. But this is not your
problem. For you, the problem focuses on impossibility.
You, the perfect Stoic with your arguments against laughter.

Tell me: how could I forget the woman on the fire-escape
with her knowledge of men, rubbing sun-lotion
            into her thighs.
I need to know what lives she's involved in, the rooms
she might live in. Yet I pretend I'm only interested
in the distance from a to b. I laugh.

Look for the common denominators! No matter
that you are a failed mathematician! No matter
that your teachers thought you innumerate!
Be confident! Two and two never equalled four!

I know it's useless; all that's certain is our manipulation
of these distances. Our exile is self-imposed. We assume
            the features of stone.
September in Lyon's Tea Shop. The sky over Huddersfield
            in ruins.

On the Nature of Discourse

Polemics in Marxism are common-place
the discord only natural.
So it is adequate to note
that Professor Burnham opposes

Marx's dialectic on the grounds
of crude determinism, and with it
the historical necessity of anything
especially socialism.

When asked by Professor Novak:
Don't you think you will die some day
and isn't it absolutely necessary,
or do you think you might be immortal?

Professor Burnham replied
with logical consistency:
my death is not absolutely necessary
and certain; it is only extremely probable.

Poem Towards the Acquisition of Patronage

Queen Elizabeth, it's the same old story,
my gutterings and Edwardian drainpipes are leaking;
my mistress has left her husband
and taken off with another man;
the age of chastity has surely passed
and the waiting millions are still not happy.

Queen Elizabeth, the story's not so complicated,
old uncertainties have given way to new;
can't you chastise the whisperings
of your servants who call you Brenda;
won't you wipe out the rumours
of your stinginess with charity.

Queen Elizabeth, the story's never flattering,
and I'm not well up on court etiquette
but your "Anus Horribilis"
is cropping up on everyone's tongues;
can't the poet laureate swing the people,
the court painters paint away your troubles.

Queen Elizabeth, the story only gets worse;
we are drawn to the past like children
drawn to the edge of the tallest buildings;
will your corgis defend the palace gates
against the masses who only wish to see
the erotica in your private collection.

Empress of soap, arbiter of grief, love of the age,
dressed in tinsel and nostalgia,
here it comes again, raising its ugly head,
prancing and cavorting down the aisles
like an impostor at a princess's wedding
or an intruder in a royal bedroom...

I'm just an old-fashioned boy
who can't say no -
my heart's in a terrible spin
and just for good measure
an infinity of light sources
are poking fun at the sky.

Footnote

In modern Russia there is talk of restoring a Tsar;
the surviving Romanovs wait with baited breath,
mesmerized by their sense of fate. Throughout
Europe duty calls. All the old houses are waiting,
the little boy Grand Duke Giorgi is no exception.

What must he make of it all, his ancestors shot
by the Bolsheviks, the seventy years of 'communism',
and now this, his grand tour of Ekaterinburg?
What must he make of the commotion in the square,
the brutal words of his cossack defenders?

Sverdlov shot the Tsar! Pull him down! Kill him!
Once again the sky is darkening over Ekaterinburg:
the Priesthood waves incense like candyfloss
before the guns of the riot police; the would-be Tsar,
little Giorgi, can only look bewildered by it all.

Yacob Sverdlov looks on unmoved by the squabble.

Lunch Hour

In St Peter's gardens, the young sunbathe
on well kept lawns. Office girls hitch their skirts up,
rub protective lotion into their thighs. Passers-by
pretend not to notice, but workmen in their plastic
hats on the church scaffold, whistle and grunt between
bites. Round the edges the paths are paved with grave-
stones. Some of the names are indecipherable. I wonder
if anyone else has noticed, how soft the ground is.

Notes From The Art Underground

1

It is said that Van Gogh's ear
could distinguish the sound

of sunflowers rustling
from the sound of irises;

even at twenty paces
it is argued that the chattering

of irises is something
to write home about.

If you sit quietly enough
you can hear them growing.

2

Furthermore, it is maintained
that the ear still searches

for Gaugin and lost love,
that loneliness is all

in the mind, that Van Gogh's
mind was unstable, and the ear

although elusive in later work
found it's way into the post

time and again. Ladies and gentlemen
of the jury, the ear was famed

for its lonely disposition
yellow skies and blue fields.

3

But, if you turn the lights out
colour dissipates.

In some sense, it is like
having the wool pulled

over your eyes, a colloquialism
for being duped. However,

sitting in the dark
can be just as revealing.

It is well known that some of us
prefer it that way.

4

This at least is certain;
it is easy to feel your way

round a piece of sculpture.
Who hasn't had their paws

on the arse or tits
of a bit of marble or bronze.

It is well documented
in the history of sexual fetishism -

the distancing. Inanimate objects
are known to induce orgasm.

What is less easy to accept
is moles listening to paintings.

The Grinder

after the painting by Diego Rivera

Grind. Grind. Grind. Always grinding. Love:
Do you see
how thick my arms have become?

I have worn the stone
to a gentle curve

with my thick arms. Always rolling,
never needing, while you indulge yourself

on the front porch, talking with your comrades
(a rowdy bunch the lot of them)

about your revolution. *Emiliano!*
Do you notice
how rough my hands have become;

and me the eldest daughter
of one of the finest families in Guadalajara?

My dress the only dress I own (shame say it)
is in tatters, so much so now

that I'm afraid to show my face at market.
Every day I straddle the stone,

my arse in the air
to the prevailing winds

and all I hear is your talk of the proletariat,
"what is to be done" and "why" -

how you belong to the people;
how your people will provide bread

for *the* people, etcetera and so on,
until I'm at a loss for what to think.

Grind. Grind. Grind. Always grinding.
My love:
I grind for you and the revolution,

but these nights when I lay awake,
exhausted by the day's events

I can't help wondering
what will be,
what will finally become of us.

Woman in the Green Jacket

after Auguste Macke

Our lovely Edwardian virgin
certainly looks striking in green; however
one needn't be shocked by the fact
or feel irreverence, that our heroine -
only daughter of the right reverend Norbut Joy,
although well into her twenties (twenty-nine
to be precise) still dreams of being taken
in the silence of the rhododendrons;
and who could blame her, after all
the question still lingers on all our lips
like the effulgent gossip of washer-women
at the mangle, the necessary ontology,
the figuring of grief: will the tinker ever return
as promised on that fateful day by the lake,
when he pushed his luck under
the picnic blanket, not to mention his hand
beyond the call of duty,
beyond the deliberations of petticoat love,
over and under, into the green yonder of folds
of that magnificently buttoned jacket?

La Belle Romaine

in the model's voice

I can't listen a moment longer to your theories about adultery,
your ramblings about love. The world of intrigue no longer exists
for me. I won't get on all fours, not even for you Modigliani,
        not even for the sake of art.
Every day we perform these rituals, the same childish games,
but today is different. Today I come to the studio a stranger,
a refugee in my sandled feet, bleeding little puddles which drain
        through the floorboards.
Poor Modi! The pretence is finally over! Michel has left me
for a girl called Tammy and all I can do is run.
I'm running away from this city of duplicity, where schoolgirls
        are too easily fondled into bed.
I used to love Paris in the Autumn, but now the rain has lost
its charm. No amount of rain can assuage the city's bored tears,
or the mess I find myself in. The rain is lost on both of us,
        we are both lost in the rain.
At night, I dream of the river, gurgling through the city.
I see it from the studio window, washing through the streets
of Montmartre. I'm alone in bed, and the Seine
        is collecting debris for the sea.
When I wake up, the sheets are soaking. Some nights I feel
as though I'm drowning. Such is the nature of departures!
Such is the nature of love! Old love departs for new,
new love for old,
        or no love at all.
Sometimes it just departs. Unsure of everything, like the concierge
in her high chair on the floor below, watching the water
drip from the ceiling, seep through the cracks in the wall,
        collect in pools at her feet.

The Gypsy Lovers

after Otto Müller

Love's young dream courts perfection by the lake

understanding little or nothing
of transience, they embrace and kiss
playful as children under the linden trees
on the edge of the forest;
though there are no boats on the surface
or for that matter any discernible water
in the painting - it all exists
like amaranth or instances of joy
without refrain or the need for qualification -
they would not have it any other way;
he gives her the stars; she gives him her thighs;
we cry in our various reticences:
love is not love unless it hurts!

Woman in a Fish Hat

after Pablo Picasso

We are well acquainted with your public
life; inside us all the terror is waiting,
the private tragedy we do not talk about,
people and places we cannot share.

You're right; scars never mend, they grow
less visible, seem less real, the days fold
into one another like paint - grey
into black - but remain inquisitive,
we want to know more. We want details.

You say it's not possible. It cannot be said.
And we are sad because you have fallen
silent, your hands knotted as if in pain,
your breasts struggling under canvas,
under the weight of that Fish Hat.

Tixall Road

This is my present to you.
It is a painting of a man and a woman
in a rented bathroom.
The man is shaving.
The woman is washing her hair.

Each day the past month,
I have lugged the image of it
from pub to pub
in my drunkenness,
talking all the while to strangers
about oil paint and poetry.

I say to them, imagine yourself
in the painting, there
among the white-washed walls
and pumice stone, there
where the breeze cools
the water's skin,
hardens breasts and nipples.

If only you could see it now,
the goosebumps and the sun
pouring all day;
if only it wasn't wrapped up
like this, awaiting
the final touches, you'd see
how peaceful the scene is.
How simple.
How unlike worry.

A Bigger Splash

after David Hockney

Nothing moves in the eleven o' clock sun, not even the splash.
      It is July and
the deck chair casts the self-same shadow it has always cast.
      Beyond the east
facing windows, everything is certain. The palm trees out back
      do not anticipate
wind. The grass stationed against the east wall of the apartment
      does not expect
rain. Nor do the windows ever expect to be opened. In the blue
      geometry
of water and sky, the matrix of flatness and suspension denies
      feeling.
There is no impropriety; no leaves in the pool; nothing doing
      except for
the splash, meticulously detailed; and so it is; only the splash
      with its eternal
whooshing that makes the implausible possible.

End Of History

The party leadership extolled
the virtues of the West, they
appealed to the people, arms
outstretched, their hands held

as if in prayer: To get rich
is glorious! We must learn to swim
in the ocean of the commodity
market! In the distance, tanks
                              moved
about like cattle over the cobbles.

Chips With Bits

Caught between the tired looks
of a woman too busy to smile
and the queue, longer than usual
for this time in the evening:
a boy of twelve, embarrassed
by a poverty he thinks is unique,
mocked and bullied by children
who tell him it is, seeks his
reflection in the polished
steel of the counter and hates.

Diogenes Searches for Foundation

for David Morley

Sceptics say the window is intangible.
I don't doubt it. Modern alchemy (science
if you like) is the stuff of fairy tales.
However, I am blameless. I never pretended
any progress towards truth, the window
is only a nightmare for the sleepless;
dependent on, yet independent of the subject.

Forget history! The invisibility of the atom
is at stake. I only excavate the past
to rid myself of tiresome artefacts.
To prove my point, I've given up the barrel
for a room of glass, not nearly as comfortable.
I can't deny the difficulties involved;
the nights of research leave me glassy eyed.

And though my dreams have become disturbed
since I took to dreaming syllogisms,
the results are quite satisfying. Up to press
I've found there are three types of people
in the world; those who throw stones
at lab windows, those who don't, and
those who are permanently skating on glass.

Of course there are set-backs, the unconscious
mind is reluctant to allow for valid logical form.
Last night I stumbled on a world without sand,
a world without windows, wild flowers, grains
of any description; then the dream shrunk
from me, and I woke in a glass room, no bigger
than a demijohn, no more significant.

I could go on for an age like this, except
the critics are crowing about testability.
I must get back to my step ladders, chammy cloths
and random variables. I can't keep away
from the window with its lack of certainty,
how, if shattered, it might resemble the universe:
broken glass, spiralling down an infinite regress.

Prometheus Depressed

O.K. I'm downright nasty at times,
especially just before breakfast;
what do you expect, with that damn bird
preying on me all the time and the ocean,
the damn Aegean forever spraying
salt into my wounds. (His words ring out
over the cliffs.) I'm sick to the stomach
of this crumbly anxiety, sick
of waking every morning with the vulture
at my liver - it's knackered anyway.

O Fortuna, imperatrix mundi!
Who really cares about the suffering
of others - the gods? Don't kid yourself.
My one regret. I only ever wanted to be normal.

Uncle H

It is quite possible, then, that Hector
deceives himself with visions of love,
trinkets, amulets, photographs - all junk,
all of it carried from pillar to post,
the assemblage of a secular life;
when, what he sees, is the fallen ankle
of obsession, bleeding in its sandled
glory, bloated on the field of regret;
lying, lying, lying, like weathered bone,
anaemic against the whitening sky.

That's uncle Hector alright, always one
for the grand negative. Poor uncle H,
busy creating his own disturbance,
stares at his shield, abandoned in the sedge.

Threnody

Despite Ariadne's protestations
on Hector's behalf, vis à vis the Minotaur's
habitual hunger - good words are hard
to come by; and Hector knows this,
primarily, because the heart
of the Minotaur, whose business (really)
is eating princesses - isn't easily won;
despite all the known facts about what is
reasonable; for example: it is
reasonable to believe that one will not
be gobbled up for din dins by a beast,
half man, half bull; the Minotaur -
(the bastard) simply cannot find it
within himself to be reasonable.

Minotaur Fabula

The Minotaur is not all monster.
The Minotaur suffers great sorrows.
The Minotaur is no doubt an aesthete.
The Minotaur is a creature of habit.
The Minotaur loves his labyrinth.
The Minotaur has feelings too.
The Minotaur fears his own shadow.
The Minotaur hates his own shadow.
The Minotaur questions his own reason.
The Minotaur worships Ariadne.
The Minotaur is a sucker for love.
The Minotaur is a glutton for punishment.
The Minotaur is at best unreasonable.
The Minotaur is after all half human.

Uncle H at Knossos

I have dreamt all the best poems, never written
them down, except the odd line scrawled
on the walls of the labyrinth.
Never the chance, met most days by the sound
of builders and labourers busying
themselves with bricks and mortar, as the wall
is raised ever higher, until thoughts
of escape return once again to thoughts
of enclosure. This is my world
of sensory deprivation. Walls and Parapets.
Parapets and Walls. Where touching hurts.
Touch is alien. Yet it is touch alone that counts.
And the poem written is like Daedalus
regretting the decision to fly.

Orpheus in-love

1

Caught once again calling her name,
caught once again with his pants round his knees,
caught once again hoping for her return,
caught once again asking the obvious,
caught once again berating the cruel fates,
caught once again unable to sleep,
caught once again lamenting the fact,
caught once again throwing salt about,
caught once again with his head in the jar,
is pilloried by his contemporaries,
who, for the main part, remain sober:
Stop crying over unfair reality!
(they shout) It exists the way it exists!
And you'd do well to bloody well accept it!

2

But our hero, pitiful in his loss,
(being rather sceptical at times)
asserts, that reality no more exists
than the fears of what we cannot know,
or the drinks for which we cannot pay
and simply won't rest until she's restored:
Goddess! Siren! Girl of nineteen years!
What man wouldn't feel it in his bones -
a woman like that! Alas poor Orpheus!
anacreontic to the bitter end, loves
what he cannot love, lives for what
he cannot live, and will no longer sing,
(since all his singing is given to doubt)
drinks himself stupid at every turn.

Kojak Eulogy

This is not Kojak.
This is New York without any hope
        of resurrection.
This is New York seen from the air.
This is a poem about a painting of New York
        only insofar as it exists in the poem.
This is a painting then, without lollipop love.
This is New York breaking away,
        Floating away out into the Atlantic, towards Europe.
This is the New World meeting the old.
This is New York without meaning.
        Kojak is no more. Who loves you now, baby?
This is New York, meaner and tougher than ever.
        No-one can sleep easy in their bed.
This is New York in mourning, finally
        fragmenting.
This is a poem for Kojak, a lament
        for Jacques Derrida.
This is the trash can of history, mouth gaping
        salivating, urging monsieur Derrida
        to accept his fate.
        This is New York.
        She is dressed in black.
        Kojak is dead.
        She is inconsolable.

Funeral Party

When the hours of morning stop and dawn forces
its greyness, the dead will come to your bedsides
as strangers, carrying their mirrors like lanterns.
They will gatecrash the skulls of the heaviest
sleepers, leave them with nothing, want nothing,

not even regret. Hear this! I am the last guest
to leave, the last chief of the gooney birds, mindful
of my responsibilities, mind full of excuses. Listen
to the sea for no other reason than it is there.
Listen so long as listening matters. I have strayed

a thousand miles off course, left my nesting grounds
to the stone men and come among you to let you share
this sense of loss. Hooray for the excesses of the ego!
I want my fifteen minutes of fame, my claw prints
on the sidewalks of Hollywood. Cut me and I bleed.

Peck at me with your beaks. Peck at these eyes
until they are as blind as the sun. The problem
remains. Half-four; the sun at its brightest
lights the room, demands meaning.

Ceremony

Walking the hours hoping
that rain could displace regret,
the further I walk the more obvious
it becomes; if there is a constant
it's the knowledge that you're not
coming back. I'm like the man on the road
gang waiting for rain to clear,
the man on the platform wanting
to jump, arriving early, hoping
the train will be late.
I rush into a phone box with no one to call
and nothing in mind except relief
from the rain, only to find
the air rotten. I could argue
the phone was an enemy
to communication. But it doesn't matter,
tonight, I cannot deal with ghost
conversation. I've finished
with self-justification and the dividing
of blame. It could have worked
and then it couldn't. One last poem,
that's all I wanted to give you;
one last poem with regrets too numerous
to assemble.

The Tin Cat

We are at war, me and the cat
with the kids next door.
If you hadn't already noticed
I'll spell it out.
My cat is made of tin.

It has red fur and black eyes
and not the other way round.
It lunges at passers by
and nosey parkers and isn't
in the least bit superstitious.

The neighbours think
there's something strange
about a kid with a lump of tin
but the joke's on them.
We don't care what they think.

All morning we've been diving
through their privet, making holes
for fun while they're out at work.
Our philosophy is simple.
They've had it coming for ages.

Like I said. Tin cats are the best.
They don't like nosey parkers
because nosey parkers are like mice.
And they don't like other cats
especially cats in poems.

This is tin cat alley, keep out
if you know what's good for you.

Mark Murphy was born in 1969 and lives in Huddersfield. He studied philosophy at Staffordshire Polytechnic, and is presently studying for his MA at Huddersfield University.

His poem 'Footnote' won 2nd prize in the National Militant Labour Poetry Competition 1994.

Also available from Spout Publications:

You What? by John Bosley
Piltdown Man and Batwoman by Milner Place
The Chrysalis Machine by Steve Littlejohn
A Little Book of Leaving by Stuart Rushworth
Perfect Legs by Dianne Darby
Dancing Fish by Michael Wilkinson
Shall I? by Susannah White